Straight from the Soul

Straight from the Soul

Claire-Louise Osorio

ISBN: 9798515763466 (Paperback)

Physical edition printed by Kindle Direct Publishing.

First printing edition 2021.

Front cover image by Freddie Finn.
Book Design by Will Mancini.
Illustrations by Jenny Wren.

www.foreverphoenix.blogspot.com

SHADES OF BECOMING:

MERGING WITH SHADOWS   3

STEPPING INTO LIGHT   34

ACKNOWLEDGMENTS   75

This book is dedicated to my paternal grandmother, Eveline. Her wonderful poems and stories, recited aloud and from memory, were the highlight of the long summers of my childhood. I believe that her gift for language is something that I have inherited; so, this one is for you grandma.

Straight from the Soul

MERGING WITH SHADOWS

"I love you as certain dark things are to be loved, in secret, between the shadow and the soul."

— Pablo Neruda

"I like weird people... The black sheep, the odd ducks, the rejects, the eccentrics, the loners, the lost and forgotten. More often than not, these people have the most beautiful souls."

— Unknown Author

The Melancholy Moon

Just as the waning crescent moon
might lament the loss
of her once resplendent fullness,
so too I mourn those parts of me
that have been lost.

The childlike innocence
that made me trust without question,
the open heart that felt no need
to guard and defend against the perils of love.

And just as the waning crescent moon
might glimpse her own pale, diminished form
in the mirror of the sea
and feel a longing to return to wholeness,

I yearn to rediscover that
carefree girl I used to be.
Before life's troubles transformed me
into a dull reflection of my former self.

You Will Never Know

You will never know
how silently
the words you said
shift and turn inside my head,
as sleep eludes
my restless eyes.

You will never know
how tenderly
the faded petals
of a yellow rose,
unfurl the lingering imprint
of your gentle smile.

You will never know
how vividly
the echoes of the past are stirred,
by half-forgotten melodies,
whose music floods
the silence of an empty room.

You will never know
how violently
the tender memories
of mother and daughter
on a Paris street,
unstitch my heart and halt my feet.

You will never know
how ferociously
my love for you endures,
unaltered by the steady march of time,
by shifting landscapes and changing climes...
unbroken and unbreakable.

A Magnificent Machine

A magnificent machine
turned against itself,
enslaved by torturous ruminations.

The unconscious mind
creates its own reality,
believes its own inventions.

In this fearful space
dark thoughts take root,
like weeds in fertile soil.

Extinguishing hope,
suffocating joy,
feeding on fear.

Freedom lies
beyond the grip
of memory and imagination.

In conscious presence
internal dialogue subsides,
and mind can rest in peaceful stillness.

A Self-Fulfilling Prophecy

Fear grips my heart
like a vice,
at the thought that one day
you might not think twice,
about leaving me for her...

That faceless woman
just beyond the horizon.

The taunting echo
of these voices in my head,
haunts me most
when I go to bed,
as my restless brain
sifts through memories…

For 'Evidence'
to fuel my fear.

This anxious mind
tries hard to keep me safe,
from being hurt and losing faith.
Instead, it builds
a walk around my heart
that slowly pushes us apart.

Until one day I wake up
and you're gone…

The Mirror Soul

Born just 11 days apart,
but separated by continent and culture.
When eventually they met,
their eyes betrayed the weary look of soldiers,
with hearts already hardened
by countless battles, lost and won.

Lovers and adversaries,
at times they rode the waves
of pure, ecstatic bliss.
Until love's sweet tide abruptly turned,
then 'till the bitter end they fought,
with words like shards of glass, precision aimed.

Catnip or kryptonite,
they were each other's sweetest elixir
or most bitter poison.
Heaven or hell, dark or light,
no shades in between.

Inexplicable but unbreakable
their bond endured,
no matter how far or fast they fled.
Twin flames bound by an invisible thread,
their souls conjoined
long before they ever met.

Impossible Love

You talked of love
but my heart could not hear it,
I talked of love
but your mind made you fear it.

Always at odds
the timing so wrong,
but this bond of ours
stayed unfailingly strong.

We were once great lovers
then my body grew cold,
its warmth turned to ice
by wounds new and old.

We tried to be friends
but time could not erase,
the taste of our kisses
or their lingering trace.

Twin flames born to be together
but so often forced apart,
caught in a battle
between head and heart.

Pride became our enemy
mistrust our greatest foe,
but this love will endure
wherever we go…

Sleepless Nights

Many nights
I have wept,
on the pillow
where you slept…

A wayward drummer
playing havoc
with the steady beat
beneath my breast.

Lying here
upon our bed,
your parting words
inside my head…

Like jagged shards
of glass,
piercing hope,
puncturing joy.

I wonder how
a love so strong
could turn to dust
and make us wrong.

The Guarded Heart

The guarded heart dwells inside a fortress
designed to defend and protect,
with armed sentinels at every point.

The guarded heart shields itself from others
by launching verbal missiles, sharp as knives,
at anyone who gets too close.

Behind an impenetrable drawbridge,
raised high to exclude and enclose,
the guarded heart lives in fear and solitude.

But somewhere deep within the darkness,
the guarded heart hides a secret longing,
far stronger than fear, much greater than pride.

A yearning to be broken open,
defences shattered, ramparts destroyed,
so that from the smouldering ruins…

A brave new being may emerge.

The Innocent Captive

You tore me down
with verbal missiles, artfully aimed
to punch the air from my lungs
and bring me to my knees.

But even after I regained my feet,
traces of your brutal words remained
imprinted on my heart, embedded in my soul
etched in indelible ink on my memory…

Where they put down poisonous roots
and spread seeds of self-doubt.
Until nothing could dislodge them
from my troubled mind.

Observing my distress,
you decided to change tack
and play the hero,
charging to my rescue.

And so, you built me up again,
with empty praise
and grandiose declarations
of love everlasting.

Then, with masterful trickery
and false promises
designed to flatter and coerce,
you skilfully entrapped me.

Feeding me just enough
of the good stuff
to ensure I wouldn't catch a glimpse
of freedom, just beyond the bars.

Sharp Edges

Your words became embedded
in my memory,
like tiny shards of glass
beneath my skin.

But just when I thought
I had removed
the last piercing fragment…

A hidden splinter,
fragile as a cobweb in the wind,
brought tears to my eyes again.

A Letter to My Ex

Thank you for showing me
what I didn't want,
so I could see more clearly
what I do want.

Thank you for failing
to make me happy,
so I could learn to create
my own happiness.

Thank you for not valuing me,
so I could pay attention
to all the ways
I wasn't valuing myself.

Thank you for betraying me,
so I could learn to trust
the precious gift of intuition
over the seductive lure of empty words.

Thank you for holding up a mirror
to all my self-limiting beliefs,
so I could stop playing small
and start revealing my light to the world.

Thank you for breaking my heart,
so I could finally learn
not to give it away
so hastily next time.

Thank you for the lessons…

Moment by Moment

I am living my life
one moment at a time,
breathing as steadily as I can
to stem the rising panic
in my chest.

Your sudden departure
from my world
has shaken me to the core,
leaving me
unsteady on my feet.

The unceasing hum
inside my head
ensures that sleep
continues to evade me,
as darkness gradually
gives way to light.

At night, my mind replays
the final scene
of our last encounter
on a repeat loop,
unwilling to let go.

Some days the tide of my grief
feels like it may turn,
as the sting
of your absence
begins to recede.

And yet my mind rebels,
dragging me once again
into that hellhole
of *Ifs, Buts* and *Whys*.

These relentless thoughts
make me feel like a madwoman,
desperately seeking water
to quell the blaze
inside her head.

So I am living my life
moment by moment,
breath by breath,
heartbeat by heartbeat,
one day at a time... until I break free.

Turn the Other Cheek

"Turn the other cheek,"
they said.
"Rise above it,"
they advised.

And yet,
of this truth I feel sure,
there are times to be still
and times to take action.

To rise up and reclaim
our warrior spirit,
just as our feisty forebears
would have done.

For though our modern world
may seem quite secure,
this is no Paradise.
And in this realm of fallen angels
it pays to stay alert...

As there are those
who would rob and cheat us,
break our hearts
or leave us for dead.

These are things my Mama
never taught me,
so I learned them the hard way
in the harsh school of life.

Not everyone is my friend,
not everyone can be trusted,
and not everyone was raised
as she raised me.

So I will save
my politeness and respect
for those whose smiles
match their intentions.

But if some dark soul,
whose shifty eyes betray
the urge to harm,
should cross my path…

I will bare my teeth
and hold my ground,
like a fearless She-Wolf
defending her cubs.

The Changing Face of Beauty

Just as petals
fade to grey,
it seems that beauty
has its day.

Good looks that once
enchanted all,
no longer make
the menfolk drool.

Her skin reveals
her years on earth,
her body changed
by giving birth.

Yet in her eyes
it's plain to see,
the playful girl
she used to be.

Despite the mirror's
mocking stare,
of her own worth
she's now aware.

The silver streaks
amongst her hair,
the self-assurance
of her stare…

These things can only
come with age,
but she has learned
to love this stage.

She's ready now
to live her life,
not as a mother
or a wife...

But as herself
forever free,
to become the woman
she yearns to be.

The Woman in Black

Dressed in black from head to toe,
her skin as fair as falling snow,
she sits straight-backed against the chair,
her face half hidden by her hair.

She's done her makeup with great care,
but something in her absent stare
hints at a loss she cannot share,
a burden she alone must bear.

As I watch, she lifts one hand,
on which I glimpse a wedding band.
The row of diamonds catch the light,
their rainbow colours shining bright.

Perhaps she's a widow,
who can say?
Her closed expression gives nothing away.
Those watchful eyes of forest green
do not reveal what they have seen.

From time to time, she glances up,
and taps her fingers on her cup.
Then she takes a mirror out,
and draws herself a scarlet pout.

With steady gaze she scans the room,
it seems she's waiting but for whom?
She has a story, there's no doubt,
that she alone knows all about.

As time ticks by I watch her face,
but of her feelings there's no trace.
The mask she wears a perfect guise
to hide her thoughts from prying eyes.

The Alchemy of Loss

No longer anyone's daughter,
no longer a wife,
I am cast adrift
in a strange new life.

The anchor of family
has been taken away,
and this unwelcome solitude
gets lonelier by the day.

But the truth of impermanence
is something we all have to learn,
and destiny has decreed
that for now it's my turn.

So I'm using my alone time
to learn to love me
as this is the path
to become truly free.

Pachamama

Pachamama,
Mother Earth,
to you we owe everything
including our birth.

But how we've mistreated you
pains my soul,
as our short-sighted greed
has taken its toll.

The once pure air is
now choked with fumes,
but despite all the damage
we continue to consume.

As though your resources
were ours to expend,
we exploit your treasures
for our own selfish ends.

Yet this sudden pandemic
and it's widespread effect,
has given us time
to pause and reflect.

Now many have realised
we can't live this way,
and changes are needed
to keep disaster at bay.

Finding Freedom

In loving you
I sometimes lose myself,
my deepest needs
neglected on the shelf.

But over time,
I've come to see
that my first duty
is to me.

So when I feel
I've nothing left to share,
I take the time
to practice some self-care.

For truth be told,
I cannot be a *We*
until I've learned
to take some time for me.

These precious moments
on my own
have taught me
how to be alone.

To reconnect
with my own heart,
and not feel sadness
when we part.

For love begins
with loving me,
and with this insight
I feel free.

The Misfit

You did your best
to raise me well,
but I seemed alien to you.
An ugly duckling,
trapped in a nest
built for another.

My unwillingness
to hide my truth,
to play by the rules,
puzzled and frustrated you
in equal measure.

I tried so hard
to make you proud.
But soon the truth revealed itself…
the more I tried,
the emptier I felt.

Until one day, I learned
to be proud of myself,
for never giving up,
for honouring my truth,
and spreading happiness
where I could.

The Wisdom of the Phoenix

When the pain comes,
let it bring you to your knees.
Offer no resistance,
let it rage through you like a hurricane.

Let your body go limp,
and your mind go still.
Attach no 'story' to this unfolding,
just let it be what it is:
raw, visceral pain.

Remain in sweet surrender
as this Phoenix process unfolds,
consuming and destroying
all in you that has to die.

Trust that nothing has been lost
but that which had to go.
Bask in the stillness,
as you breathe out the old,
inhale the new.

Witness the majestic unfurling
as the Phoenix lifts its mighty wings,
and slowly rises from the ashes…
the miracle of life reborn.

A Sacred Birthright

I used to feel that love
was something I must chase,
a privilege I had to earn.
As if being loved
were not my sacred birthright.

Those I chose to love
were willing participants
in my dark delusion.
They let me do all the work,
tie myself in knots to please them.

But my best was never good enough,
and they let me know it…
withdrawing their affection
until I tried harder, gave more,
expected less.

Eventually, the more I gave,
the less I received.
Until my heart felt hollow
as an empty shell,
cast adrift on an ebbing tide.

And then, at last, I understood:
this was not love
but love's dark underbelly…
a projection of my shadow self,
those parts of me I had disowned.

No longer looking for love
where it would never be found,
I learned to give myself,
what I was seeking.
And, with that, my shackled soul broke free.

Stepping into Light

"To confront a person with his own shadow is to show him his own light."

— Carl Jung

"Your task is not to seek for Love, but merely to seek and find all the barriers within yourself that you have built against it."

— Rumi

Re-Writing Her Story

She rewrote the story of her past,
one chapter at a time.

Until a tale of mere survival
became a testament
to the strength and resilience
of her unbreakable spirit.

The Rise

With unflinching courage,
she boldly entered
the circle of fire
and let herself burn.

And as the flames consumed her,
those aspects of herself
that did not serve her highest calling
reduced to karmic ash.

Until nothing was left
but her shining soul,
pure and indestructible
as a diamond.

And then, with grace,
she spread her wings
and began to rise…

The Maverick

Always the odd one out…
the one who didn't talk enough,
or talked too much
at the wrong time.

The one who asked awkward questions,
never accepting anything as true
until she could verify it for herself.

The one who felt too much
and sometimes let her emotions spill out,
embarrassing others.

The one who shielded her ivory skin from the sun
when it was fashionable
to have a tan…

And kept her dark tresses long,
when convention dictated
that women her age should wear it short.

A square peg in a round hole,
she contorted herself into unnatural shapes
in a bid to be accepted.

Until one day she learned to embrace
her own unique otherness…
and with that she grew wings.

The Light Bearer

Her mind didn't always follow
the linear flow of logic,
perhaps that's why she found it so hard
to toe the line.

The Black-Sheep,
The Outcast,
speaker of inconvenient truths
that others found uncomfortable.

She shone her light
into dark corners,
revealing things that many
would have preferred
be kept hidden.

Look Up

Look up
into the ever-changing sky.
Observe the shifting pattern
of the clouds...
A reminder that
in this world
nothing stays the same.

Look up
at the trees,
inhale their earthy scent.
Listen to the rustle of their leaves,
and attune your ear
to their whispered wisdom.

Look up
at the birds
as they soar on high,
watch how effortlessly they glide and dip.
Imagine the world
viewed from above...

And when your thoughts get too loud,
or your sense of self too big,
remember this:
we are but a tiny speck
on the surface
of a vast globe.

Seeing Through New Eyes

To her eyes,
Family was a word
that spelled just one thing:
Trouble.

To heal her heart
and start anew,
she put an ocean
in between herself and them.

But though she discovered
new places and faces,
life still followed
the same cheerless script.

However far or fast
she fled,
the spectres of the past
always tracked her down.

Until one day
she fought the urge to run,
and bravely faced her demons…
one by one.

But though they wailed
and gnashed their teeth,
the more she stood her ground
the faster they retreated.

Until she learned
to trust her strength,
and self-doubt turned
to self-assurance.

And through the alchemy
of fierce self-love,
the shadows of the past
became a guiding light...

A beacon in the darkness
showing her the path
back home,
to her true self.

So she began
the journey of a lifetime,
without setting foot
beyond her own front door.

A Love Note to Myself

Remember, you are the honey
so let the bees come.
There's no need to chase
love or approval.

Just focus inwards
to find your own bliss.
That way, nothing external
will ever make or break you.

Wild Woman

Fearless,
untameable,
free as the wind,
strong as the trees.

She needs no introduction,
her presence announces itself.

She wears her wild curls proudly,
like a symbol of brazen self-acceptance.

She lives in harmony with the seasons
and the changing rhythms of her body.

She eats when she feels hungry:
heartily, unapologetically.

She laughs from her belly,
and loves with her whole soul.

But when she feels pain,
she howls like a She-Wolf
beneath the harvest moon.

She answers to no one,
instead, she lets herself be guided
by the age-old wisdom
of instinct and intuition.

The Gift of Love

Breathe in love,
breathe out fear,
as we lie here
ear to ear...
The outer world
fades away,
and no harm
can come our way.

In your arms
my heart can rest,
as my head lies on your chest.
No greater stillness,
no deeper peace,
next to you
my worries cease.

Until this time,
I never knew
how life would change
on finding you.
Or just how easy
love could be,
with someone who
would set me free.

To be myself
no questions asked,
in perfect stillness
two souls unmasked.

The Rhythm of the Tides

The inhale
and exhale
of the sea,
the most blissful music
there could be.

To ears attuned to nature
such as mine,
this sacred sound
becomes a portal
to the Divine.

As when I sit and listen
to the tide,
I find that place of peace
that's always there on the inside.

The part of me
that's forever still,
beyond the ever-changing
dictates of my will.

The Ever-Changing Self

A Russian doll
of many selves,
inside this woman
a young girl dwells.

Playful and joyous,
she's the fun part of me.
The one who sings loudest
and feels the most free.

But sometimes the woman
who's been battered by life,
takes over my head space
and causes me strife.

These different personas
appear to be real,
but their transient nature
another truth must reveal.

So who is this *I*
that I think of as me,
and which of her faces
reflects reality?

The self that I sense
when my thoughts become still,
and my mind is unshackled
from the force of my will…

Tells me that I'm not the body
or even the mind,
but the silent observer
who exists beyond time.

Love Laid Bare

When everything seems
bleak and dark,
and life itself
a touch too stark…

In your eyes
I see the spark
that lifts my mood
and fills my heart.

Since meeting you
I've learned to dare,
to live each day
without a care.

To lose my fear
of standing square,
my heart exposed
my fair skin, bare.

You've been my rock
on stormy days,
and soothed my soul
in many ways.

Whilst in your arms
I've felt your gaze
upon my face
like warm sunrays.

Friend and lover
you've taught me how,
to drop the past
and live the now.

And in your presence
l can see,
the carefree girl
I used to be.

The Seer Within

Deep within me dwells an ancient seer,
who *sees* without seeing,
hears without hearing,
and *knows* without knowing,
all that lies beneath material form.

This is the uninvited messenger,
whose late-night whisperings
stir me from sleep,
urging me to attune my inner ear
to the wise oracle within.

When I am lost,
this is the voice that leads me home.
When I have doubt,
this is the map that shows me the way,
the direct route to my own North Star.

This is divine consciousness,
my compass for the soul…
Guiding me to know the *unknowable*,
see the *unseeable*,
and hear the *unhearable*.

Living a New Reality

Breathe in life force, hope, inspiration.
Breathe out fear, anxiety, despair.
As you inhale the new,
exhale the old.

Let go of all your relentless striving.
Observe the steady beat of your own heart.
Attune your ear to the vibrations of Mother Earth,
let her age-old wisdom return you to yourself.

Find new ways to bridge the distance.
Drop into stillness, connect with your heart.
From this place of sacred centredness,
send waves of pure love to those you hold dear.

Let go of who you thought you were…
Release judgement, expectation, the need to control.
Feel the pure air caress your skin,
embrace the stillness of a world reborn.

Words of Wisdom
to the Girl I Used to Be

Don't try so hard for love,
there is nothing you need do.
Those who know your value
will need no persuasion.

Don't try so hard to fit in,
in seeking to be accepted
you will only lose yourself.
Live by your own truth.

Don't try so hard to be liked,
strive only to like yourself.
It's not your business
what others think of you.

Don't worry so much about your looks.
Embrace your perfect imperfections,
wear them with pride,
hold your head high.

Don't be led by the crowd.
Follow your intuition,
trust the silent knowing
you hold inside.

Don't believe all your thoughts.
Watch them as they come and go,
some kind, some cruel,
changeable as the weather.

Don't take yourself so seriously.
Be light,
be playful.
Embrace the gift of youth.

Making Friends With Fear

As 2020
sheds its skin,
making way for
a New Year to begin…

My mind returns
to these twelve months past,
to find some wisdom
that will last.

I ask myself what
I too must shed,
to quieten the fears
inside my head.

They have a name these
uninvited guests,
but I've come to see them
as friends, not pests.

For they let me know
when I'm off track,
yet their doom-filled messages
no longer hold me back.

I greet them with a smile,
and in giving them a name,
I've denied them the power
to cause me pain.

Let me introduce you,
if I may,
to Merciless Maggie
Despondent Dora, and Calamity Kay.

These clamorous women
have good intentions at heart,
but in keeping me safe
they also keep me apart...

From my greatest self
and the dreams I hold dear,
patiently awaiting me
on the other side of fear.

So now when I hear them,
I simply say:
"Thank you for sharing, but come what may
I choose to have faith that I'll be OK."

A Lover's Vow

I intend not to fall,
but to relax deliciously
into love.

To drop my guard
and reveal my soul
slowly, inch by inch…

To that lucky one,
who has earned
my loyalty and devotion.

I intend to love
with eyes wide open,
but without trepidation.

With no fixed agenda
or past story
to cloud the present.

I intend to love
with no need to defend
or pretend...

Honestly
Fearlessly
Joyfully…

Ancient Goddess Moon

As I gaze
upon your face,
I feel the presence
of pure Grace.

Your timeless beauty
makes me swoon,
my heartbeat drums
to your sweet tune.

Your shifting aspects
hold the key,
to something deep
inside of me.

An age-old wisdom
that may be,
your gift to all humanity.

For though your form
may seem to change,
as you move
through wax and wane…

Your basis essence
stays the same,
and all that alters is your name.

And so with us
this fact holds true,
eternal nature through-and-through.

Lessons from the Virus

Shut all your doors,
but not your heart,
in these dark times
when we must stay apart.

Do not let this virus
steal your joy,
take this time
to redeploy.

Focus your mind
on what matters to you,
and don't let the news stories
make you feel blue.

Savour the small things
and you will see how,
practicing gratitude
keeps your mind on the now.

You've been here before
so there's no need to fear,
make use of the wisdom
you've gained in this year.

Reach out to your loved ones
to tell them you care,
and despite social distancing
find new ways to share.

By standing together
we can weather this storm,
and rise from the ashes
like a creature new-born.

The Dance of Love

Let there be space
in our togetherness,
and togetherness
in the space between us.

Let us dance to the rhythm
of this merging and diverging
in perfect equilibrium.

Let love be the constant
within the ever-changing,
undiminished by the shifting tides
of time and circumstance.

And after all our restless wanderings,
let love be our sanctuary.
That blissful place we call home.

The Secrets of the Sea

As I sit and watch the sea,
a certain insight comes to me…

That as the shifting tide does show,
how breaking waves both come and go,
so too our lives will ebb and flow.

For nothing ever stays the same,
and after joy there's sometimes pain.

But of this truth we shouldn't fear,
for without darkness they'd be no light,
without the hard times, no need to fight.

And in this battle we've come to see
how strong we are, and will always be.

Letting Go

You taught me to relax into love
and live the present moment,
in all its glorious fullness.

Like a tender rose,
whose half-closed petals
unfurl beneath the morning sun,

I turned towards
the steady warmth of your gaze
and let my fears release…

One by one,
until I stood
exposed before you,

Allowing you to see
the girl in me
I had kept hidden,
lest she seem

Too intense,
too emotional,
too complicated.

But you just smiled
and embraced all of her
with love and understanding,

And, with that,
I saw reflected in your eyes,
the wondrous image
of my own perfect imperfection.

Flourishing

Love used to bleed me dry,
but in your arms
I've found my home.

Now the spiky walls
around my heart
have begun to crumble and fall...

And flowers are growing
in the cracks.

From Darkness to Light

I watch in reverent silence,
as the night gracefully gathers up
her dusky skirts
and retreats to the wings.

Whilst somewhere on the eastern horizon,
the Star of the show
unfurls his amber cloak,
before taking centre stage.

As darkness gives way to dawn,
I tilt my face skywards
in silent anticipation…

Catching my breath
as the first rays of light
flood through the half-closed shutters
of my weary soul…

Melting the ice
in my heart
and warming
my chilled bones.

As a new day unfurls,
luminous as a fresh-water pearl,
I slowly breathe out…

Allowing all the tensions
of the long sun-starved months
to ebb slowly from my body.

In Memory of Eve

We knew you as Eve
and to my young eyes,
when they handed out grandmothers
I got the prize.

A weaver of tales
and a spinner of yarns,
your words had me spellbound
like magical charms.

A tale of two creatures
was a favourite of mine,
so I knew it by heart
by the time I was nine.

A vain white rabbit
and a dim-witted mole
were abruptly acquainted
when she fell in his hole.

She begged him for help
so he prayed for her soul,
whilst her beautiful fur
slowly blackened like coal.

Decades have passed
since I last saw your face,
but your wonderful stories
leave an indelible trace.

To those who loved you
as dearly as me,
these treasures now form
your legacy.

A Futile Quest

Perfection does not exist,
and yet my stubborn mind persists
in striving for a goal
that does not serve my soul.

For truth be told
it's nothing but a lie
that often stops me
before I even try.

So for today
I'll choose another thought
to free me from this trap
in which I'm caught...

And no longer give a damn
if I'm not perfect as I am.

For I am worthy
even with my flaws,
and this sweet truth
is also yours.

Emerging

To eyes grown accustomed
to empty streets
and vacant doorways,
this colourful panorama
fills my soul with glee.

Everywhere I look there is movement:
frisky dogs with tails on high,
lively children giving chase,
parents strolling hand in hand,
their thoughts elsewhere.

Tables lined with happy punters,
drinks in hand, faces upturned,
as busy waiters cruise between them
balancing their overladen trays.

To ears grown accustomed
to months of steady silence,
the joyous babble of carefree chatter
sounds like the sweetest melody.

And as the setting sun
spills her amber rays upon me,
my heart swells with jubilation
for life feels almost 'normal' once again.

The Mirror Moon

In the lunar cycles of
endings and beginnings,
fullness and emptiness,
I see the ever-changing pattern of my life.

But just as the waning crescent moon
does not lament the loss of
her once resplendent fullness,
I embrace each new phase with joy.

I am indebted to several people for the creation of this book and it is thanks to their unwavering support that you, my readers, are now holding it in your hands.

Firstly, I would like to thank my editor, Will Mancini, for his patience, vision, and razor-sharp editing skills.

I would also like to thank my illustrator, Jenny Wren, who has skilfully translated the images in my head into the beautiful illustrations within these pages.

Finally, I would like to thank my partner Elliott Mercer, who has both encouraged and inspired my writing.

Claire-Louise Osorio is a linguist with two degrees in modern languages from the University of London. She lives in Dorset on the South West coast of England with her partner Elliott, and Buddy the three-legged cat.

This is her first published book of poems, but she has been writing both poetry and prose in the form of short stories and other narratives since 2011. Many of these can be found on her blog:

www.foreverphoenix.blogspot.com.

This edition of
Straight From The Soul
is designed by Will Mancini. The
typeface used in the interior is
Garamond and Times New Roman.
The typefaces used on the exterior are
Modernline and Times New Roman.